THE SUMMER AFTER THE CHRISTMAS WHERE WE DID THAT THING WE SHOULDN'T HAVE

A one-act comedy by
Brent Holland

www.youthplays.com
info@youthplays.com
424-703-5315

 ISBN 978-1-63932-053-0.

COPYRIGHT RULES TO REMEMBER

1. To produce this play, you must receive prior written permission from YouthPLAYS and pay the required royalty.

2. You must pay a royalty each time the play is performed in the presence of audience members outside of the cast and crew. Royalties are due whether or not admission is charged, whether or not the play is presented for profit, for charity or for educational purposes, or whether or not anyone associated with the production is being paid.

3. No changes, including cuts or additions, are permitted to the script without written prior permission from YouthPLAYS.

4. Do not copy this book or any part of it without written permission from YouthPLAYS.

5. Credit to the author and YouthPLAYS is required on all programs and other promotional items associated with this play's performance.

When you pay royalties, you are recognizing the hard work that went into creating the play and making a statement that a play is something of value. We think this is important, and we hope that everyone will do the right thing, thus allowing playwrights to generate income and continue to create wonderful new works for the stage.

Plays are owned by the playwrights who wrote them. Violating a playwright's copyright is a very serious matter and violates both United States and international copyright law. Infringement is punishable by actual damages and attorneys' fees, statutory damages of up to $150,000 per incident, and even possible criminal sanctions. **Infringement is theft. Don't do it.**

Have a question about copyright? Please contact us by email at info@youthplays.com or by phone at 424-703-5315. When in doubt, please ask.

CAST OF CHARACTERS

ELLA, any gender, the killer. Nice and well-liked, but holding on to a lot of rage.

EMILY, female, quick to panic.

SARAH, any gender, levelheaded and friendly. Was against the plan from the beginning.

CHARLOTTE, any gender, bossy and strong-willed.

HALIE, any gender, easygoing and funny.

AVA, any gender, mature. A leader among the group.

ROCCO, any gender, Jackson's best friend and quick to joke.

JACKSON, any gender, laid-back. Rocco's best friend.

COLBY, any gender, decisive and quick to action.

MALIK, any gender, everyone's friend. The person who states the obvious.

JACOB, any gender, usually serious and usually found with Nick.

NICK, any gender, impulsive and quick to act.

Note: Almost all of the characters are flexible in gender, with the possible exception being Emily. and if you choose to switch that, feel free to change the names of any characters to fit the actor you cast in the role. All characters are high school seniors who have recently graduated.

SETTING

An upper class living room in a house on Melton Island, a private vacation spot.

(When the lights come on, EMILY, SARAH, CHARLOTTE, HALIE, AVA, ROCCO, JACKSON, COLBY, MALIK, JACOB and NICK are entering a nice living area decorated for Christmas.)

CHARLOTTE: This is really nice, Halie!

SARAH: How many bedrooms has this place got?

HALIE: Six. So, everyone has a roommate. The pool is heated, and there's a poolhouse in the back.

MALIK: What's up with the Christmas decorations?

HALIE: I don't know. I guess Uncle Eric spent Christmas here and hasn't been back yet.

NICK: *(Picking up a decoration and doing a Tiny Tim impersonation:)* God bless us, every one!

EMILY: I say we leave it up—I love Christmas.

COLBY: I do too, just not in June.

ROCCO: *(Looking at his phone:)* Reception is really bad. I don't have a signal at all.

HALIE: I was just looking at that. It's never great, but I usually have a couple of bars.

MALIK: Nothing at all on mine.

NICK: Does anyone?

(They all check and see that no one has a signal.)

HALIE: I'm sure it won't be like that all weekend.

JACOB: Who cares? We have our own island for a weekend!

HALIE: Well, not really… We only own this one plot.

JACOB: But the other two houses are empty! No one's home! This is awesome.

EMILY: I'd still like to have my phone… I told Ben I'd call and text, ya know?

HALIE: It won't be like this all weekend, I'm sure.

(ELLA enters.)

ELLA: Sorry, took a wrong turn coming up. *(To Charlotte:)* Your dad hadn't left yet, so I'm good.

CHARLOTTE: Great!

JACKSON: Do you have any cell reception, Ella?

ELLA: *(Looking at her phone:)* None. *(To Halie:)* Is that normal?

HALIE: No, but I'm sure it's just the weather or clouds or something.

ELLA: Is it a good idea staying here if we can't contact the mainland?

AVA: I'm sure it will be fine.

JACKSON: Is there a landline?

HALIE: I think there was one years ago, maybe.

AVA: It will be fine!

MALIK: It's probably only temporary anyways.

HALIE: Well, let's put our stuff away and go swimming!

NICK: The bedrooms are all upstairs, right?

HALIE: Three on the second floor and three on the third.

JACOB: I want a room on the third floor!

(Jacob exits to claim his room.)

NICK: I'm rooming with Jacob!

(He exits.)

SARAH: Thanks for setting this up, Halie.

HALIE: I can't imagine a better way to spend graduation week!

CHARLOTTE: I can't believe we're done with high school.

ROCCO: I've known most of you since elementary school.

JACKSON: And next year we won't be at the same school together.

ROCCO: Or even the same state, for some of us.

COLBY: So, let's make this an exclamation point on our high school years.

MALIK: Yes!

ELLA: I have a feeling that this is going to be the best weekend ever!

(Blackout. When the lights come back up, all twelve teens are sitting around. Some have phones out, some are snacking. There is a thunderstorm going on.)

ROCCO: I couldn't eat another thing.

JACKSON: Me either.

AVA: Swimming all day made me hungry, but yeah...I'm stuffed.

CHARLOTTE: Thanks for cooking, Ella!

ELLA: I'm happy to! I looked in the pantry, and it has all kinds of weird food.

COLBY: Like what?

ELLA: Cornish hens, canned goose, just a lot of stuff like that.

HALIE: Uncle Eric lives in London for a good part of the year, so I guess that's what they eat there.

MALIK: *(Looking at his phone:)* I haven't had reception all day.

AVA: And you thought that would change during this thunderstorm?

(Thunder.)

EMILY: I kind of like the thunder.

NICK: Me too. This is cool.

JACKSON: This is the first time I've ever been through a thunderstorm with Christmas decorations up.

ELLA: I think we should plug in the tree!

CHARLOTTE: Good idea!

ELLA: *(To Colby, who is already standing:)* Plug in the tree!

COLBY: Sure.

(He goes to plug the tree in.)

NICK: This puts me in the mood for eggnog.

SARAH: Yuck—you like that stuff?

NICK: Love it.

JACKSON: Eggnog's pretty polarizing: People either love or hate it.

MALIK: I've never had it.

NICK: Never?

MALIK: Milk allergy.

EMILY: That's right. You always had to get water at lunch because of that.

MALIK: Something in milk makes everything swell up. Eggnog smells pretty gross, though, so I figured risking my life to try it was a bad idea.

NICK: That makes sense. Your loss, though—that stuff is righteous.

COLBY: *(Noticing a sign on the CD player:)* Hey, there's a note here.

CHARLOTTE: A note?

COLBY: It has all of our names on it.

EMILY: What does it say?

COLBY: It just has all of our names. It has a CD in it.

EMILY: A CD?

COLBY: It was sitting next to this CD player. The CD has "play me" written in marker.

HALIE: *(Laughing:)* Which one of you put that there?

(They all deny it as a group.)

NICK: Well, put it in the player.

COLBY: OK.

(He does, and a dark, ominous voice plays.)

OMINOUS VOICE: Welcome to Melton Island.

MALIK: Thanks!

(The rest shush him.)

OMINOUS VOICE: On December 3rd of this year, twelve high school students conspired to steal the Douglas P. Hernandez High School Christmas Fundraiser money. The twelve of you are guilty of stealing more than 5300 dollars that would have been used to help fund the Parker Homeless Center.

HALIE: How does he know about this? Which of you told on us?

OMINOUS VOICE: That money, which would have helped feed children and families through the holiday season, was wasted by the twelve of you on your own selfish desires.

ELLA: I didn't tell anyone!

OMINOUS VOICE: You thought you got away with it. You thought you would never have to pay for your crimes, but judgment day has arrived. You have all been found to be on the naughty list.

NICK: I bet it was Charlotte!

CHARLOTTE: Me?

OMINOUS VOICE: Each of you will pay for the Christmas cheer you stole from the less fortunate. None of you will leave this island alive.

EMILY: What does he mean by that?!

(At this, "The Twelve Days of Christmas" starts to play. After a few moments of the tune, the teens start to argue.)

CHARLOTTE: One of you told someone we stole that money!

HALIE: It wasn't me!

SARAH: I never wanted to go through with it. You all know that!

JACKSON: You could have put an end to it at any time!

JACOB: I still have no signal.

EMILY: We can't call for help!

HALIE: Calm down, Emily!

EMILY: *(Building:)* Calm down? That creepy voice just said that none of us are going to leave this island alive!

MALIK: When is your dad picking us up, Charlotte?

CHARLOTTE: Monday, after lunch.

EMILY: We'll all be dead by then!

JACKSON: No, we won't. We'll be fine. Is this a joke? Is one of you playing a joke on us?

HALIE: We swore each other to secrecy. Did any of you tell anyone?

(They all indicate that they didn't.)

JACKSON: Can someone turn off that stupid music?

(Colby goes and turns off the CD. A moment passes.)

EMILY: This can't be happening.

NICK: Jacob, go to our room with me.

JACOB: Why?

NICK: I want to get something out of my bag.

JACOB: Did you bring a gun?

NICK: A gun? No. Why would I? I have something else, though.

(Nick and Jacob exit.)

ELLA: You shouldn't go off by yourselves.

JACOB: *(As they are leaving:)* We'll be fine.

CHARLOTTE: I'm hungry.

JACKSON: What? How can you be hungry?

CHARLOTTE: When I'm stressed, I want to eat.

JACKSON: There's no reason to be stressed. Seriously. One of us is playing a joke here.

HALIE: It's not a very funny joke.

CHARLOTTE: I'm going to get some chips.

(She gets up.)

HALIE: I'll go with you.

(Charlotte and Halie go to leave.)

(To the others:) We'll be right back.

ROCCO: I thought it was the perfect crime.

SARAH: There are no perfect crimes.

ROCCO: *(To Sarah:)* You didn't snitch us out, did you?

SARAH: Me? Why would I?

ROCCO: Because you didn't want to do it.

JACKSON: Yeah…you totally tried to talk us out of it.

ROCCO: And we literally made you take your share of the money.

SARAH: Which is why I would never snitch us out. I'm as guilty as you are.

ELLA: She's got a point.

EMILY: I feel like I'm going to throw up.

COLBY: It's going to be OK, Emily. We're going to be fine.

EMILY: We can't call for help, and we can't leave the island, and there's someone here that wants to kill us.

JACKSON: We don't know that.

MALIK: We don't?

JACKSON: This could be a joke.

ROCCO: Or maybe someone found out and they just want to scare us.

EMILY: That doesn't make any sense.

COLBY: None of this makes sense.

ELLA: I have to use the bathroom. Which one is the closest?

AVA: The one right down the hall.

ELLA: Be right back.

(Ella starts to exit.)

EMILY: Don't go!

ELLA: I'm just going down the hall, Em. I'll be back in thirty seconds.

ROCCO: You pee quickly.

ELLA: You know what I mean. I'll be fast.

(Ella exits.)

MALIK: This sucks.

AVA: That's the understatement of the year.

EMILY: We are so screwed.

JACKSON: Could you chill?

EMILY: Shut up, Jackson.

JACKSON: Panicking won't help.

EMILY: *(Starting to panic:)* Are you serious?

JACKSON: What?

EMILY: We should ALL be panicking. If we all panic, then we are all taking it seriously.

COLBY: Just because some of us look calm doesn't mean we aren't taking it seriously. We're going to get through this, Em.

EMILY: I'm scared, Colby.

(The lights go out.)

That's not helping!

MALIK: The lights are out.

ROCCO: Ya think?

(Nick and Jacob enter.)

NICK: Who turned out the lights?

ROCCO: Malik did.

MALIK: I did not!

JACOB: The power's out.

AVA: Do we have any candles?

EMILY: I really, really don't like the dark!

COLBY: Calm down and help us find some candles.

(Ella enters.)

ELLA: Not funny, guys, I can't pee in the dark! *(Realizing:)* Oh—the lights are out in here too.

JACKSON: We're looking for candles.

NICK: Isn't there a breaker box in the hall?

ELLA: There is.

NICK: *(Exiting to find the breaker box down the hall:)* I think it's right over here.

MALIK: *(Turning on his flashlight:)* My battery is low. Hopefully the lights come back on.

(Charlotte enters.)

CHARLOTTE: Did the lightning knock out the lights?

(Her cell phone flashlight is on.)

JACOB: We think so.

CHARLOTTE: Do we have candles?

EMILY: Can this possibly get any worse?

(The lights come back on. Halie is dead in the middle of the floor with a drumstick protruding out of her back. For a moment, no one notices.)

MALIK: The lights are back on.

ROCCO: Thanks for the update.

EMILY: Thank God. I was about to totally freak out.

(She sees Halie's body on the ground and starts screaming.)

(Nick enters.)

JACOB: I thought you said you were about to freak out!

(Emily points as she screams, and everyone sees and immediately backs up from Halie's body.)

MALIK: That's Halie!

ELLA: Is she dead?

ROCCO: Hey, Halie! Hey! Are you OK?

JACKSON: Don't you see the blood?

ROCCO: Blood doesn't mean she's dead!

AVA: Should we touch her?

(Emily screams again, scaring them.)

NICK: Don't do that!

EMILY: Halie's dead!

NICK: We don't know that!

AVA: Someone should touch her and check.

ROCCO: Halie! If you are OK, could you say something?

(Jackson goes up to her and prods her with his foot. He takes a step back in fear. He gets closer.)

JACKSON: Hey, Halie... *(He looks closer:)* I don't think she's breathing.

(Emily screams again, scaring them all.)

NICK: Stop doing that!

COLBY: *(Pulling Emily away as she cries into his shirt:)* Calm down, Em.

(Jackson kicks Halie again.)

JACKSON: I think she's dead.

CHARLOTTE: Oh crap. What do we do?

ELLA: We need to make sure.

CHARLOTTE: Does she have a pulse?

JACKSON: I don't know.

CHARLOTTE: Check!

JACKSON: I don't want to touch her!

JACOB: Just do it!

JACKSON: I'll do it.

(Jackson walks up as the others back up. He checks her pulse by touching the back of her head.)

I don't feel anything.

AVA: That's her skull, moron. Feel her neck.

JACKSON: I didn't think it mattered. *(Touching:)* Here?

(Ava nods.)

OK. I don't feel anything.

MALIK: This really sucks.

JACOB: What do we do now?

(Malik grabs his phone.)

MALIK: Hang on.

JACOB: What are you doing?

MALIK: I'm going to… *(Realizing.)*

ROCCO: No reception, doorknob.

CHARLOTTE: Should we move her?

COLBY: Move her where?

CHARLOTTE: I don't know. Somewhere else.

AVA: Are we allowed to move her?

ELLA: I don't know.

ROCCO: What is that sticking out of her?

(Jackson pulls it out.)

SARAH: Don't pull it out!

JACKSON: Already did.

SARAH: Put it back in!

(He stabs it back in Halie. Everyone is grossed out.)

MALIK: That's nasty.

ROCCO: What is it?

JACKSON: It's a drumstick.

ELLA: A drumstick?

JACKSON: *(Looking at her:)* And she's been stabbed a bunch.

SARAH: How can you tell?

JACKSON: There are holes. Stab holes. *(Counting:)* Someone stabbed her thirteen times.

EMILY: Oh my God.

NICK: Thirteen times?

JACKSON: Yeah, thirteen. *(Thinking:)* No—actually twelve. I stabbed her once.

SARAH: Does this mean that the person that stabbed Halie was a drummer?

ELLA: Maybe.

CHARLOTTE: Colby, you play the drums.

COLBY: So? Do you think I stabbed Halie?

CHARLOTTE: Of course not! I'm not saying that!

JACOB: Why would someone stab Halie twelve times with a drumstick?

JACKSON: I have no idea.

CHARLOTTE: We should move her.

SARAH: I don't think the cops would want us moving a body.

CHARLOTTE: Jackson stabbed her.

JACKSON: She was already dead!

CHARLOTTE: What I'm saying is that we've already disturbed the body, and since this is the only room that fits the eleven of us comfortably, we should move her somewhere else.

SARAH: We should call the cops. Does anyone have reception yet?

(They all check, and none of them do.)

NICK: Maybe we will soon. I'm going to check the third floor. Maybe it's better up there.

JACOB: Don't go alone.

NICK: Come with me.

(They both go to leave.)

ELLA: I'm going to check my room on the second floor.

AVA: Be careful.

COLBY: I'm going to check outside. Maybe there's a spot where the signal is stronger.

EMILY: I'm going with you.

COLBY: Are you sure?

EMILY: I trust you, Colby. I want to be where you are.

SARAH: I'll go, too.

(Emily, Sarah and Colby exit. A moment passes.)

CHARLOTTE: I want to move her.

AVA: That's not a good idea, Charlotte.

ROCCO: What's that smell?

CHARLOTTE: *(Pointing at Halie:)* That's her.

MALIK: She can't be rotting already.

CHARLOTTE: That's not her decomposing, that's the smell of...

MALIK: Ew.

ROCCO: I thought that was a myth... You really crap yourself when you die?

JACKSON: I don't know about everyone, but it sure looks like Halie did.

CHARLOTTE: Help me move her.

AVA: We need to leave her here.

CHARLOTTE: That smell is only going to get worse.

(She grabs Halie's arms.)

AVA: Don't move her!

CHARLOTTE: One of you help me.

JACKSON: I'm not touching her.

CHARLOTTE: You just stabbed her!

JACKSON: That's before I knew she had dropped a load. That's gross.

ROCCO: I'm not touching her either.

CHARLOTTE: Fine—I'll do it myself!

MALIK: You have fun with that.

(Charlotte drags Halie offstage.)

JACKSON: That smell is nasty. I wonder if there's any air freshener.

ROCCO: I have a can of Axe upstairs. Be right back.

(Rocco exits.)

(A moment passes.)

AVA: It was her idea, you know.

MALIK: What?

AVA: The whole idea to steal the money. It was her idea, wasn't it?

JACKSON: Originally. She came to me with it, and we jokingly hashed it out together.

AVA: It's not so funny now.

JACKSON: I still haven't processed this. I'm not even going to try.

(A serious moment passes.)

MALIK: I wonder what she ate that would smell that bad.

(Nick and Jacob enter.)

NICK: No reception up there.

JACOB: We checked the balcony and got nothing.

NICK: Where's Halie?

AVA: Charlotte dragged her off.

NICK: Where to?

AVA: She didn't say. She couldn't take the smell.

NICK: That smell is Halie?

JACKSON: Yeah, she had the death poops.

NICK: Gross.

(Rocco enters and starts dousing the room down in body spray. After a few moments:)

JACOB: That almost makes the smell worse.

AVA: I was just thinking that.

(Emily screams from offstage.)

NICK: That was Emily!

(They start to move as Emily, Sarah and Colby enter. Colby stops them.)

AVA: What happened?

COLBY: It's Charlotte.

(Ella enters.)

ELLA: What about Charlotte?

COLBY: Someone attacked her by the back door.

AVA: Attacked her?

COLBY: She's dead.

AVA: Are you sure?

COLBY: Her head was caved in by this.

(He shows them a big metal pipe.)

SARAH: She's definitely dead.

(Emily is crying.)

COLBY: What was she doing there alone?

JACKSON: She was taking Halie somewhere.

SARAH: Why?

ROCCO: Halie was smelling ripe.

SARAH: So Charlotte thought it was a good idea to disturb a crime scene?

AVA: You know how Charlotte is.

SARAH: Was.

AVA: She's definitely dead?

SARAH: Go look for yourselves.

AVA: Come with me, Rocco.

ELLA: I want to come too.

AVA: Fine.

(Rocco, Ella and Ava exit.)

NICK: Why does it smell like a middle school locker room in here?

JACKSON: Rocco sprayed Axe to get rid of the poop smell.

NICK: Halie really pooped herself?

JACKSON: I mean, we didn't check or anything, but we're pretty sure.

SARAH: Why would anyone do this to us?

MALIK: Karma?

SARAH: I don't think karma for stealing money is a brutal, violent death.

MALIK: Maybe one of the teachers figured it out.

JACOB: And now some vigilante teacher is out to murder us? That doesn't make sense.

MALIK: Does any of this make sense?

SARAH: I can't believe Charlotte is dead.

EMILY: And Halie. I've known Halie since kindergarten.

JACKSON: We need to find them.

NICK: Who?

JACKSON: Whoever killed Charlotte and Halie.

SARAH: How are we going to do that?

JACKSON: The killer still has to be here, don't they?

NICK: I guess...

(Ava, Ella and Rocco come in looking subdued.)

AVA: You're right. Definitely dead.

ROCCO: That was even grosser than Halie.

JACOB: Who would want to take a piece of piping like that and...

ELLA: Wait...piping...

JACOB: What?

ELLA: Eleven pipers piping!

MALIK: What?

ELLA: From the song that was playing: "The Twelve Days of Christmas"!

ROCCO: What does that have to do with Charlotte?

ELLA: Don't you see it? Eleven pipers piping and twelve drummers drumming!

COLBY: Twelve drummers?

MALIK: Halie was killed by a drumstick!

SARAH: And that song played at the end of the message we got!

ELLA: It's just like the song!

ROCCO: It could be a coincidence.

SARAH: Impossible! That song was playing on the CD!

JACOB: You think that someone killed Charlotte and Halie so that it fits with "The Twelve Days of Christmas"?

ELLA: I think it's definitely possible. Charlotte was killed with a pipe… Eleven pipers piping!

JACOB: That's pretty sick.

NICK: Jackson thinks we should look for the killer.

AVA: Why?

JACKSON: To get him before he gets us!

ELLA: How are we going to do that?

JACKSON: I say we split into pairs and search every room of the house. Whoever finds them calls out, and the rest of us will come running.

ROCCO: I'm in.

NICK: Me too. Someone definitely wants all of us dead.

COLBY: It was only 5300 dollars! Why would someone do this?

JACKSON: Are you in?

COLBY: Of course I am.

EMILY: Me too.

JACKSON: OK. We need to split up, but I want two people to stay here to be central if one of the other groups finds him.

COLBY: I can do that.

SARAH: I'll stay with him.

JACKSON: That works.

ELLA: I'll take Emily, and we'll do the third floor.

EMILY: I don't know...

ELLA: Come on, Em, I won't let anything happen to you.

EMILY: *(Hesitantly:)* All right...

(Emily and Ella exit.)

NICK: *(Indicating Jacob:)* We'll take the second floor. If I find the killer, I've got something for them.

(He pulls out a collapsible baton.)

ROCCO: Where did you get that?

NICK: Got it from my bag after Halie was stabbed. You never know when you're gonna need backup.

ROCCO: What if the killer has a gun?

NICK: If that's the case, I hope your group finds him.

ROCCO: Thanks.

NICK: Come on, Jacob. Let's get this over with.

JACOB: Now I feel like I need a weapon.

NICK: *(Picks the pipe up off the ground:)* Here—take this.

JACOB: *(Without thinking:)* Thanks.

MALIK: Dude, that's got Charlotte's brain junk on it.

(Jacob drops the pipe.)

(Looking down:) Now the brain junk is on the carpet.

JACOB: Hmm.

(He picks it back up and wipes the pipe on the couch.)

SARAH: What are you doing??

JACOB: Cleaning the pipe.

(He inspects it.)

Looks good now.

MALIK: Remind me not to sit on that couch.

(Nick and Jacob leave.)

AVA: Malik and I will take the rest of this floor.

MALIK: Can we do somewhere else?

AVA: Why?

MALIK: Because down the hall there…

AVA: What? It's just Charlotte and Halie.

MALIK: Yeah, but they're dead.

AVA: And?

MALIK: You don't see a problem with that?

AVA: I'll search the hall if it bothers you.

MALIK: Now you're making me sound like a wuss. Fine, whatever. Let's go search right next to the freaking dead people.

(Malik and Ava exit.)

JACKSON: Rocco and I will take the yard. If you hear us call, come running.

COLBY: Be careful out there.

SARAH: It's raining really hard.

ROCCO: This is going to suck.

JACKSON: Let's get it over with.

(Rocco and Jackson exit.)

SARAH: *(After a beat:)* You know, I never wanted to steal the money to begin with.

COLBY: I remember. I didn't either. I tried to play sick from school the day we did it, but my mom totally flipped on me for trying to miss school.

SARAH: I didn't know that. Why did you go through with it?

COLBY: I didn't want to let down my friends. Why did you?

SARAH: I didn't feel like I could say no to them. I never felt right about it, though.

COLBY: Me neither.

SARAH: I did do something about it, though.

COLBY: You did? What?

(From a distance, Emily screams.)

COLBY: Emily!

(Immediately Colby and Sarah sprint off upstairs. After a few moments, Rocco and Jackson enter in a hurry.)

JACKSON: Colby! Where are you?

(Malik and Ava run in.)

AVA: Was that Emily that screamed?

ROCCO: Had to be.

JACKSON: They're on the third floor.

(They are about to run upstairs as Colby enters with his arm around Emily. Ava, Nick and Jacob are with them.)

MALIK: What happened?

EMILY: It's Ella...

JACKSON: What about Ella?

EMILY: She's gone!

(Emily starts crying.)

JACKSON: How? And what do you mean by gone?

EMILY: We were looking in separate rooms.

JACKSON: You were supposed to stay together!

EMILY: I know, but Ella wanted to split up to go faster. She thought the killer might escape if we weren't fast. I was searching my room when I heard something fall down the hall where Ella was. Then I heard her.

SARAH: Heard her?

EMILY: I heard her cry out. I ran to the room, but when I got there…

COLBY: *(Explaining:)* We found part of her shirt ripped and hanging on the balcony.

MALIK: What does that mean?

EMILY: Someone threw Ella off the balcony!

ROCCO: Doesn't the balcony face the rocks? That's got to be a fifty-foot drop.

AVA: At least.

JACKSON: Are you sure she fell?

EMILY: Either that or she was teleported away by aliens! She's not up there, Jackson!

COLBY: It's too dark to see if her body is down by the rocks.

JACKSON: I'm going to make sure she's not still up there.

EMILY: She was thrown out the window, Jackson!

ROCCO: I'll go with you.

(Jackson and Rocco exit.)

COLBY: I'm going to look down by the rocks. Maybe she hit the water.

SARAH: I don't think that's possible.

AVA: It's dark out there, and with the rain, you're not going to be able to see anything.

COLBY: We've got to do something... Ella could be out there. I'm going to check.

NICK: I'll go with you. I'm lifeguarding this summer. If she's in the water, I can get her out.

COLBY: Good idea.

SARAH: I'm going, too.

(Colby, Sarah and Nick exit.)

EMILY: *(After a moment:)* This isn't happening...

AVA: Try to stay calm, Em.

EMILY: I swear I'm going to slap the next person that tells me to stay calm.

AVA: It doesn't help.

EMILY: I don't care. You say it again, or if ANYONE says it again, they're getting hit.

JACOB: *(Sniffing:)* I think I've finally gone nose blind to the Axe smell. Why does Rocco even wear that stuff?

MALIK: I was thinking the same thing.

AVA: I hope Ella's all right.

EMILY: Me too.

AVA: She's always so nice.

JACOB: I can't imagine why anyone would want to hurt her.

AVA: You know she volunteers at the soup kitchen on Saturdays?

MALIK: Yeah. She doesn't talk about it much, though.

AVA: Do you think she could have survived that fall?

EMILY: Maybe she hit the water.

AVA: Maybe.

MALIK: My phone's dead. What time is it?

EMILY: *(Looking at her phone:)* It's 11:30.

MALIK: It's that late? It's weird—I'm not tired at all.

JACOB: Adrenaline does that.

MALIK: I guess so.

(Rocco and Jackson enter.)

JACKSON: She's not up there.

ROCCO: If she is, she's the hide and seek queen.

EMILY: That's not funny, Rocco.

ROCCO: Your opinion is noted, Emily.

MALIK: I thought it was kinda funny.

ROCCO: *(To Emily:)* See?

JACKSON: While we were up there, we were thinking, though. Ella being thrown out the window fits the song.

AVA: It does?

ROCCO: Yeah, "On the tenth day of Christmas my true love gave to me…ten lords a-leapin'."

MALIK: I don't get it.

ROCCO: Ella *(Using finger quotes:)* "leaped" out the window.

MALIK: Never mind—I get it now.

AVA: You think that's what it means?

JACKSON: It makes sense to me.

JACOB: It's kind of a stretch, but if Ella was thrown out the window, it could be considered a leap.

MALIK: Even though she's not a lord.

(They look at him.)

Just sayin'.

EMILY: *(Ignoring Malik:)* This is just so evil.

JACKSON: Stating the obvious is Malik's job.

EMILY: Up yours.

MALIK: Yeah, up yours!

AVA: Can you all just shut up?

EMILY: I can't deal with you right now. I'm going to my room.

(Emily goes to leave.)

MALIK: Good luck not getting killed! I'll be staying right here.

(He sits on the couch.)

EMILY: *(Stopping in her tracks:)* Damn it! I can't do this.

MALIK: Feel free to go upstairs and get whacked.

EMILY: Shut up, Malik.

MALIK: Yeah, yeah.

EMILY: Also, you're sitting in Charlotte's brain junk.

(Malik jumps up.)

MALIK: Gross! Yuck.

(He goes to the wall and wipes his back on it.)

(Sarah, Nick and Colby enter all wet.)

AVA: Did you find her?

COLBY: We couldn't see. The rain is raining too hard.

SARAH: *(Pulling out a wallet:)* We found this, though.

MALIK: That's Ella's wallet! *(Realizing and looking at Jackson:)* I just did it again, didn't I?

JACKSON: You totally did it again.

EMILY: Where did you find it?

NICK: On the rocks, not quite to the water.

ROCCO: So maybe Ella's still out there?

SARAH: If she is, we can't see her.

COLBY: The waves are really crashing… If she fell near the water, she could have been dragged out to sea.

SARAH: We're going to check again in the morning, once the sun's up.

JACOB: What do we do until then?

NICK: I say we stay in this room. No one goes up to their bedroom.

AVA: I can't imagine sleeping anyways.

(The lights flicker out again.)

EMILY: *(After a moment:)* Great! I freaking hate the dark.

COLBY: Calm down, Emily.

(Emily slaps him.)

What was that for??

EMILY: That's what's going to happen to each and every one of you people every time you tell me to calm down from now on. Got it?

JACKSON: OK... Did we ever find the candles?

SARAH: I don't think so.

NICK: Everyone look around.

(They do so.)

AVA: Check the cabinets.

SARAH: Here they are!

AVA: Awesome. *(Pause.)* Does anyone have a lighter?

(Everyone looks at Jackson.)

JACKSON: Why's everyone looking at me?

AVA: Do you have a lighter?

JACKSON: I do, but that doesn't explain why you're all looking at me.

AVA: Can I use it please?

JACKSON: You guys are looking at me like I'm the guy who is always ready to smoke or something.

(He hands over the lighter.)

NICK: Or something.

AVA: *(Trying to use the lighter:)* Why isn't it working?

JACKSON: It's almost out. Keep trying.

(After a few more tries, Ava lights a couple of candles and sets them up.)

AVA: It's better than nothing.

(As she sits down, the lights come back on.)

MALIK: Sweet. Guess we don't need these anymore.

(He puts out the candles right before the lights flicker back off.)

Ooh. My bad.

AVA: *(Getting up to light the candles again [it takes several tries]:)* If the lights come back on, how about not putting out the candles?

MALIK: Sorry!

COLBY: We're in for a long night, people. Get comfortable.

NICK: We should set up a guard.

JACOB: With nine of us, we each could stay up for like forty-five minutes and we'll be fine.

AVA: I don't think I can sleep. I'll go first.

ROCCO: I don't see how any of us are going to get to sleep.

(The lights slowly dim until they are totally out. When they slowly come back up, the teens have all shifted positions and are all obviously asleep. Rocco starts to stir.)

(Whispering:) Psssttt. Who's on guard duty?

(No answer.)

Hey, I've got to pee. Who's on guard duty?

(No answer. Rocco stands up.)

Hey, Jackson, wake up!

(Rocco crosses to Jackson.)

Jackson, wake up. I have to pee. I need you to go pee with me.

(He doesn't respond.)

Seriously, dude, I've gotta go bad.

(He starts to shake Jackson, who slumps forward revealing a needle sticking out of his back. Now, much louder:)

Jackson! You've got a needle in your back! Oh crap. Everyone, wake up!

COLBY: *(Immediately alert:)* What happened?

(Everyone is rising.)

ROCCO: Someone stuck a needle in Jackson, and he's not moving!

(Emily screams.)

JACOB: Don't do that! Calm down!

(Emily slaps Jacob, knocking him into Jackson, which makes both of them fall to the ground.)

Get him off of me!

(Nick helps Jacob get untangled. Jackson is facedown on the ground in the same spot Halie previously was. There is a needle sticking out of his back.)

SARAH: Who was supposed to be on guard duty?

COLBY: I went second, and I passed it off to Sarah.

SARAH: I gave it to Rocco.

ROCCO: Holy crap! I fell asleep! It's my fault.

JACOB: Have we even checked if he was dead?

ROCCO: *(Bending down:)* Don't be dead! Please don't be dead. *(Feeling for a pulse:)* No pulse.

MALIK: There's a note on his back.

(Rocco pulls the needle out to read the note.)

SARAH: Don't do that... *(It's done.)* Well, never mind.

COLBY: What does it say?

ROCCO: The handwriting isn't so good. But it says... "Sorry guys, I had a hard time coming up with something for'nine ladies dancing,' so I just decided to stick Jackson and draw some dancers on this sticky note. I'll try to do better on the next one."

SARAH: Does it really say that?

ROCCO: Yeah, it really does. Plus, there are nine stick figure women at the bottom of the note, but they aren't drawn very well.

NICK: *(Looking at it:)* It looks like that one is having a seizure.

ROCCO: No doubt.

EMILY: Guys… Jackson's dead.

ROCCO: Oh man, and it's my fault. I fell asleep on guard duty.

SARAH: It's not your fault, Rocco.

ROCCO: If I had stayed awake, Jackson would still be here.

(There is a solemn moment.)

NICK: I just noticed something.

AVA: What?

NICK: Jackson didn't crap himself.

(Everyone sniffs.)

JACOB: That's weird.

MALIK: Maybe it's not everyone, maybe it was just Halie.

COLBY: Maybe Halie had weak bowels.

EMILY: Why does any of this even matter?? Four of our friends are dead!

(Rocco grabs Jackson by the arms and starts to drag him.)

SARAH: What are you doing?

ROCCO: Putting him with Halie and Charlotte.

COLBY: Why?

ROCCO: *(Stops:)* I don't know. *(Thinking:)* It kind of makes sense, doesn't it?

SARAH: We really aren't supposed to move the bodies.

ROCCO: *(Dragging again:)* Too late now. We can't just leave them all laying around. Plus, just because Jackson hasn't pooped yet doesn't mean he won't soon. *(To Jackson:)* Sorry, bro. No offense.

(Rocco drags Jackson off. Then, after a beat:)

NICK: Do you think maybe he could have done it?

JACOB: Done what?

NICK: Well, I was thinking... What if it's one of us?

COLBY: *(Not believing:)* Really?

SARAH: Why would one of us want to do this?

NICK: I don't know... It was just a thought. It sure would have been easy for the person on guard duty to do it.

COLBY: I don't think it's one of us.

JACOB: But when we searched the house, we didn't find anyone else.

AVA: Maybe we didn't search well enough.

SARAH: Our search was kind of interrupted by what happened to Ella.

NICK: But what if we don't find anyone? Then will you admit it could be one of us?

EMILY: I don't think that's possible.

NICK: *(Pointing to where Rocco left:)* But he was on guard duty alone...

MALIK: But it's Rocco.

EMILY: And Rocco isn't a killer.

AVA: And even if he was, he wouldn't kill Jackson.

(As if on cue, Rocco reenters, sobbing dramatically. Sarah crosses to him and hugs him.)

ROCCO: *(Still crying:)* I've known Jackson since preschool.

SARAH: I know.

ROCCO: I sat him next to Halie. He didn't really like Halie that much, and he definitely didn't dig the fact that she pooped herself, but I think he would prefer sitting next to her considering what Charlotte's head looks like.

(There is a pause as no one knows what to say.)

MALIK: Word.

NICK: Yeah.

AVA: We shouldn't be moving the bodies.

JACOB: I think that ship has sailed. We just have to face the fact that the police are going to freak out at us when they get here.

COLBY: If I live long enough to have them freak out at me, I'll deal with it.

SARAH: No doubt.

MALIK: What time is it? My phone's dead.

JACOB: 5:20.

MALIK: No point trying to go back to sleep now.

AVA: Speak for yourself. I'm exhausted.

NICK: Me too.

EMILY: I don't know how any of you can sleep after that.

JACOB: I could use a couple of hours still.

EMILY: But someone is trying to kill us!

JACOB: And we'll be more equipped to stop them well-rested.

EMILY: You guys can go to sleep if you want. I can't.

SARAH: I'll stay up. I don't think I can sleep, but the rest of you should. Emily and I will stay up.

MALIK: And me.

SARAH: And Malik. We'll keep watch.

COLBY: Are you sure?

SARAH: Yeah. If we get tired tomorrow, you guys can watch over us.

ROCCO: I just want to close my eyes and forget all about this.

AVA: Me too.

SARAH: Go ahead and get some sleep.

(Lights go down and come up as time passes.)

EMILY: I wish the power would come back on.

MALIK: We tried all of the breakers, right?

SARAH: Yeah.

MALIK: I should have charged my phone while the power was on.

EMILY: You can't call anyone.

MALIK: But I could be playing something... Anything would be better than just sitting in the dark.

EMILY: My parents are right.

MALIK: About what?

EMILY: I'm totally addicted to my phone. I would slap my grandmother for 30 minutes of Wi-Fi right now.

(They all laugh.)

SARAH: Me too.

(There is a sound offstage.)

What was that?

EMILY: It sounded like something just fell.

(A beat passes.)

MALIK: Should we go look?

EMILY: Nope.

MALIK: No?

EMILY: It came from where the others are. One of them probably just fell over.

MALIK: What?

SARAH: Rocco said he sat them up, remember?

MALIK: But what if it isn't?

EMILY: Should we wake everyone up?

SARAH: It's probably nothing.

MALIK: I'll go look and make sure.

SARAH: No!

MALIK: I won't leave the room. I'll just peek down the hall.

(He stands up.)

EMILY: Malik…be careful.

(He crosses and looks down the hall.)

MALIK: Nothing. Wait—one of their cell phones is on. I can see it lit up.

(He exits.)

SARAH: Malik! Get back here.

(A beat passes.)

Malik!

(Another beat.)

SARAH: Come with me, Em.

EMILY: I don't want to!

SARAH: Fine—I'll go myself. *(As she exits:)* Malik!

(A few seconds pass, and Sarah returns.)

I can't find him!

EMILY: What do we do?

SARAH: *(Loudly:)* Everyone, wake up!

ROCCO: What?

COLBY: *(More alert:)* Is something wrong?

SARAH: We can't find Malik!

NICK: How?

SARAH: We heard something, and he ran off to check.

JACOB: Why would he do that?

SARAH: We need to find him. Split up and look!

(They split into pairs and go off shouting his name. During this, several pass through the room, until finally they all come back.)

AVA: He's just gone!

ROCCO: But how? How long was he out of sight?

EMILY: Only a few seconds!

SARAH: He looked down the hall at Halie and the others and said he saw one of their phones on.

NICK: *(To Jacob:)* Come with me.

JACOB: OK.

(Nick and Jacob exit down the hall.)

COLBY: He has to be here somewhere!

EMILY: Why is someone doing this to us?

COLBY: Calm down, Em.

(She goes to slap him, but he ducks out of the way.)

Don't hit me. I'm sorry! Freak out if you want.

AVA: Why would Malik be stupid enough to walk out of the room?

SARAH: I don't think he meant to go more than a couple of steps.

EMILY: He was only out of sight a couple of seconds.

SARAH: We literally couldn't see him for like 30 seconds max.

(Nick and Jacob enter. No one notices that Rocco exits during this scene.)

NICK: None of them have their cell phones.

SARAH: What?

NICK: Jackson, Halie and Charlotte. None of them have their phones.

SARAH: But Malik said he saw one of their phones shining.

NICK: We searched them.

JACOB: It was gross.

NICK: No cell phones.

JACOB: He made me search Charlotte. I didn't enjoy that.

NICK: I did the other two!

JACOB: But Charlotte's head!

NICK: Halie pooped herself!

SARAH: And none of them had phones?

NICK: Nope. No phones.

SARAH: Weird. Malik definitely said he saw a phone shining.

COLBY: And you searched thoroughly? You weren't gone very long.

JACOB: I mean, we didn't strip them down or anything, but we didn't see any phones.

EMILY: Did you look in their pockets?

NICK: Jeez, Emily, we totally forgot to look in their pockets!

EMILY: Shut up, Nick.

NICK: Bite me.

(Rocco enters.)

ROCCO: Hey...the water's not working.

AVA: Where did you go?

ROCCO: I had to pee. I never went earlier.

AVA: By yourself?

ROCCO: I normally go pee by myself.

AVA: You could have gotten killed!

ROCCO: I didn't think about it. I just went.

AVA: Don't do that again.

ROCCO: OK. Fine. Was the water off earlier?

COLBY: I don't know.

SARAH: It wasn't when I went to the bathroom. I washed my hands.

COLBY: When was that? After the power went out?

SARAH: Yeah, why?

COLBY: If the house is on a pump, the power would take out the water.

SARAH: I definitely went after the power went out. It was dark.

COLBY: So someone turned the water off on us.

EMILY: I bet it was the killer.

(Everyone looks at her.)

Shut up. All of you.

JACOB: We need to get the water back on.

AVA: We do? Why?

JACOB: Because the killer must have a reason to have cut the water off.

AVA: I'm not sure that makes sense.

JACOB: It does to me.

JACOB: Want to go find the valve with me?

NICK: Nah. Let's all stay here.

JACOB: But we need to get the water back on.

NICK: No, we don't.

JACOB: If we don't, we can't use the toilets.

NICK: We can use them, but we can't flush them.

JACOB: Same thing.

EMILY: We can't flush the toilets if the water is off?

JACOB: Nope.

EMILY: Then we need to find that valve. I'm not going all weekend without flushing the toilet.

ROCCO: I'm with Emily on that.

JACOB: Then let's go find the valve and turn it back on. Emily, Rocco and I will go take care of that. You four stick together and search the house again for Malik.

NICK: OK. Good idea.

JACOB: But stick together.

COLBY: You guys do the same.

JACOB: Will do. I'm pretty sure I know where the valve should be.

(Blackout. When the lights come up, we see Rocco center stage, facedown. He is dressed crudely to look like a bird, probably a swan or other white bird. Emily, Jacob, Sarah, Colby, Nick and Ava are around the body.)

NICK: What happened??

JACOB: We went around back to check the main water valve, and I asked Emily if she could read the settings on the meter, and when we looked up, he was gone.

AVA: Gone?

EMILY: Did anyone leave the group while we were gone? You were all supposed to be searching for Malik!

COLBY: No. We were all together the whole time, right?

SARAH: Definitely. We even talked about it.

NICK: We did. No one leaves the group under any circumstances.

EMILY: Someone had to have left.

SARAH: But we didn't!

COLBY: Are you assuming one of us killed Rocco?

EMILY: Rocco didn't drown himself!

COLBY: I'm not saying he did! I just don't think it's one of us!

NICK: So, you just looked up and he was gone?

JACOB: Rocco? Yeah, he was just gone.

COLBY: How long are we talking?

JACOB: What?

COLBY: From the last minute you heard him speak until you noticed he was gone?

JACOB: *(Looking at Emily:)* A few minutes?

EMILY: If that.

NICK: Then what?

JACOB: Then we started calling his name.

EMILY: It took us a few minutes to find him.

AVA: Why is he wet?

EMILY: Because we found him in the pool.

SARAH: The pool?

NICK: *(Realizing:)* Seven swans a-swimming.

COLBY: I guess that explains why he's dressed like that.

SARAH: *(Thinking aloud:)* It's not a very good swan costume.

JACOB: I doubt the killer had much time to get it on him.

EMILY: And you four swear that no one left the group? Not even for a minute?

AVA: Not at all.

NICK: Well, except for the bathroom. But that doesn't count.

EMILY: What do you mean it doesn't count??

JACOB: Going to the bathroom totally counts!

AVA: You guys were gone for a while, and I had to go.

JACOB: Are you the only one? *(To the others:)* How long was Ava out of the room?

AVA: I wasn't the only one! Nick and Colby both went too!

JACOB: You all went?

SARAH: I didn't.

JACOB: But the other three of you left the room??

NICK: Ava went first and reported the water was back on, so then we went.

EMILY: So three of you were alone at various times.

NICK: That's what we're saying, Emily. Are you saying one of us killed Rocco?

EMILY: Someone killed Rocco!

AVA: Well, someone killed Malik too!

(There's a pause.)

SARAH: Yeah, we found Malik.

EMILY: Is he...?

SARAH: He's dead.

JACOB: How? Where?

SARAH: We found him on the balcony facedown in a bucket of milk.

AVA: Someone had knocked him out and then drowned him in milk.

EMILY: Why milk?

COLBY: Eight maids a-milking.

EMILY: Malik was allergic to milk. That must have been a horrible way to go.

NICK: I don't think there's a good way to go.

JACOB: What are we going to do with Rocco?

AVA: We shouldn't move the body.

EMILY: We already moved him. We fished him out of the pool.

AVA: Oh yeah. I guess we should put him with the others.

NICK: Give me a hand.

(Jacob and Nick drag Rocco down the hall.)

COLBY: What about Malik?

AVA: We should leave him where he is.

COLBY: That doesn't seem right.

EMILY: Well, when the police show up, at least we can say we left one body undisturbed.

AVA: Well, not totally.

EMILY: What?

SARAH: We searched him for his cell phone. It was Colby's idea.

COLBY: The others had their cell phones taken. It was a good idea. Also, FYI, Malik's phone is missing, too.

EMILY: But what does that tell us?

COLBY: I don't know!

(Nick and Jacob return.)

NICK: We sat him next to Jackson. He would have liked that.

JACOB: We were just thinking…we should try to signal people on the mainland.

AVA: How do you propose we do that?

JACOB: I don't know.

AVA: The island faces a forest.

NICK: Maybe we can flag down a boat or something.

EMILY: In this weather? Good luck.

NICK: I'm not just going to sit here and wait to die.

EMILY: I'm not going out there to waste my time in the rain.

AVA: I think I'm with Emily on this one. Let's all just stay in this room together.

JACOB: I'm for going out with Nick. Sarah? Colby?

COLBY: I think the guys have a good idea. Maybe we can start a fire?

SARAH: Probably not in this rain, but we can at least try.

COLBY: But should we really split up?

EMILY: I'm staying right here.

AVA: If I stay with Emily, it should be OK. We'll keep our eyes open.

NICK: Then let's go out there and get this done.

JACOB: The sooner the better.

(Nick, Jacob and Colby exit. Sarah goes to exit but pauses.)

SARAH: You sure you're going to be all right?

AVA: We'll be fine. You sure you don't want to stay in here with us?

SARAH: I think this could work. I think we need to try.

AVA: I understand. Good luck, Sarah.

SARAH: Come out if you see or hear anything suspicious.

EMILY: Trust me, we will.

(Sarah exits.)

They're not going to see anyone. This place is remote even when the weather is great.

AVA: I know. But if it makes them feel better.

EMILY: Plus, I'm exhausted. The lack of sleep is starting to catch up to me.

AVA: If you need to take a nap, I'll be fine being on watch.

EMILY: I can't do that to you. That's not fair.

AVA: I got more sleep than you did last night.

EMILY: But Ava...

AVA: It will be fine, Em.

EMILY: Just a short nap then. Don't let me sleep too long.

AVA: My phone's at 55 percent, so I'll be fine. I have several shows downloaded.

EMILY: If you hear anything, wake me up, OK?

AVA: Of course.

(The lights fade as Ava starts watching a show on her phone. When the lights come back up, the phone is still playing. Nick, Jacob, Sarah and Colby are all very wet. Emily appears asleep, and Ava is sitting in the chair, not moving.)

NICK: Well, Em, you were right. That was a total waste of time.

COLBY: Not only are there no boats anywhere in the water, but it's raining so hard that we couldn't even think about getting a fire started.

NICK: *(Seeing Emily is asleep:)* I guess Emily finally calmed down enough to sleep.

JACOB: *(To Ava:)* What are you watching?

(No answer.)

What are you watching, Ava?

(No answer.)

SARAH: Ava?

(Sarah crosses to Ava and touches her. Ava slumps over.)

Ava!!

(Colby, Nick and Jacob cross to Ava.)

NICK: She's been strangled!

JACOB: There's something around her neck.

SARAH: Get it off!

JACOB: I'm trying!

(Jacob continues to work.)

NICK: *(Checking her pulse:)* No pulse, and she's not breathing!

COLBY: What's on her neck?

JACOB: *(Taking them off:)* It's cloth...gold cloth. Oh my God—it's five golden rings.

COLBY: Just like in the song.

SARAH: This is sick.

COLBY: What's next? What's four?

JACOB: What?

COLBY: We should have been thinking about this the whole time. Four is what? Four calling birds?

NICK: Seven swans a-swimming, six geese a-laying, five golden rings. *(Pause.)* Four calling birds, three French hens...

SARAH: Wait, what was six?

NICK: What?

SARAH: Six! Six geese a-laying? We skipped that one. The killer did five golden rings but skipped...

(There is a beat as all four look over to where Emily is laying.)

JACOB: Crap.

(Colby crosses to Emily and rolls her over. When he does, Emily has something crammed into her mouth. She is quite dead.)

Crap!

NICK: She's dead, isn't she?

COLBY: Yeah. She's dead.

SARAH: What's in her mouth?

(Colby pulls out a toy, which is a small stuffed goose.)

COLBY: It's a goose.

SARAH: Damn.

NICK: What's it wearing?

COLBY: It's a basketball jersey.

JACOB: Why would a goose wear a basketball jersey?

COLBY: *(Deadpan:)* It's got a little number six stitched on it.

(A beat.)

JACOB: *(Shouting:)* We get it! Ha, ha! Six geese a-laying!

SARAH: Jacob…

JACOB: I'm done! *(Shouting:)* Come out and face us!

(No answer.)

COLBY: That's not how this works.

JACOB: You know, maybe Emily was right. Maybe it is one of you.

NICK: What??

SARAH: Jacob!

JACOB: When we were outside, we all split up looking for dry stuff to burn. One of you could have slipped away and done this.

COLBY: You could have too!

JACOB: I know I didn't do it, but one of you could be lying!

COLBY: We're not!

(Jacob goes to exit.)

JACOB: But I don't know that.

NICK: Where are you going?

JACOB: I'm taking my pipe and locking myself in my room until help arrives. If any of you try to come in, I'll use this on you like one of you used it on Charlotte!

(Jacob exits.)

NICK: Jake!

SARAH: Let him go.

NICK: But he'll die.

COLBY: I don't know. Maybe locking ourselves in separate rooms is a good idea.

SARAH: Is it?

COLBY: Maybe.

SARAH: I don't want to do that.

NICK: I don't either. I think we should stay together.

SARAH: Me too. Until help arrives.

(Blackout. When the lights come back on, the three are still sitting around Nick's phone. It shuts off. Ava and Emily's bodies have been moved.)

NICK: Well, that was fun while it lasted. My phone's dead.

SARAH: So is mine.

COLBY: Mine is at 28 percent, but we shouldn't use it until the power comes on, just in case we get a signal.

SARAH: Should we go check on Jacob again?

NICK: *(Shouting:)* Hey Jacob, you still alive?

(There are several stomps on the floor.)

(Shouting:) OK! We hear you!

COLBY: He should really come back down here.

NICK: He will when he gets hungry. Speaking of, I'm starving. You guys want to eat?

SARAH: I've been sick to my stomach all morning.

COLBY: I'm fine.

NICK: Well, I'm going to get something. Mind watching me go to the kitchen?

COLBY: I got you.

(Nick exits, and Colby stands in the door watching Nick in the kitchen.)

Just pick something!

(After a few more seconds, Nick enters.)

NICK: Everything is expired except this canned chicken.

SARAH: Chicken in a can?

NICK: Better than nothing.

COLBY: You know, I was thinking.

SARAH: About?

COLBY: That giant turtle raft in the pool.

SARAH: What about it?

(Nick opens the can and starts to eat.)

COLBY: I think we could use it to paddle to land.

SARAH: That's at least three miles.

COLBY: I think we could do it.

NICK: I might try if the weather was better, but that may be suicide.

COLBY: Staying here may be suicide too.

NICK: If anyone gets close to me, they are going to get a face full of baton.

(He shows his baton again.)

SARAH: I hope you're right.

COLBY: I think the turtle raft may be the way to go.

SARAH: I don't swim well enough to even think about that.

COLBY: It's stupid that Jacob is locked in there by himself. It's not safe.

SARAH: Yeah. I would prefer for all of us to be down here.

COLBY: *(Shouting up:)* Hey, Jacob! How about coming back down?

(No response.)

This is stupid! Come down here! It's a lot safer down here than it is up there.

(At this, Nick collapses. Sarah and Colby look at him.)

SARAH: Nick!

(They rush to him.)

COLBY: Nick! Speak to me.

(Nick starts convulsing.)

What's happening?

SARAH: He's convulsing!

COLBY: I know that!

SARAH: Then why did you ask?

(Nick stops convulsing and is very still.)

COLBY: He's not breathing!

SARAH: Nick!

COLBY: I'm going to do CPR.

(He lays Nick down, and as he goes to give mouth to mouth, Sarah has grabbed the chicken in a can.)

SARAH: Wait! Colby, don't!

COLBY: What?

SARAH: The chicken! It was poisoned!

COLBY: So?

SARAH: If you put your mouth on his, you'll get poisoned!

COLBY: Really?

SARAH: I think so! It makes sense, right?

COLBY: OK...good. I wasn't looking forward to kissing Nick, anyways. How did you know?

SARAH: That it's poisoned? *(Showing him:)* Look on the bottom of the can.

COLBY: It says, "Oui oui, MFers. Then there were two." Oui oui?

SARAH: It's French.

COLBY: I know that.

SARAH: Three French hens. Three French chickens. Chicken in a can!

COLBY: Jeez. I'm glad we weren't hungry.

SARAH: No kidding.

COLBY: That means... *(Shouting:)* Jacob! You're dead, right?

(No answer.)

(Shouting:) Nick's dead! Are you?

(No answer.)

Jacob's dead.

SARAH: This sucks.

COLBY: Should we go check for sure?

SARAH: Is there any way he's not dead?

COLBY: No way in hell.

SARAH: Yeah.

COLBY: Well, that settles it for me.

SARAH: What?

COLBY: Let's go get the raft.

SARAH: Are you crazy?

COLBY: Sarah, it's insane to stay here. Everyone is dead except us.

SARAH: I can't swim, Colby.

COLBY: I can. Plus, we have a raft. We can make it.

SARAH: I can't do it. I have a total fear of drowning.

COLBY: You won't drown!

SARAH: You can't be seriously thinking of doing this.

COLBY: You can't think it's a good idea to stay!

(A moment passes.)

I'm getting the raft.

SARAH: No!

COLBY: As soon as I get to land, I'll send help.

SARAH: Don't go, Colby!

COLBY: It's the only way. I'll be back soon, I promise.

(Colby exits.)

SARAH: Colby!

(Blackout. Lights come back on with Sarah sitting on the couch. There is a noise.)

Colby?

(Ella enters.)

ELLA: No, by now Colby has undoubtedly drowned.

SARAH: Ella? We thought you were dead!

(She goes to hug her.)

ELLA: You don't want to hug me.

SARAH: What?

ELLA: It would be pretty tacky for me to hug you before I kill you.

SARAH: Kill me? What?

ELLA: I've got to kill you, Sarah. To complete the song.

(She crosses to the Christmas tree.)

I put a small hole in the turtle raft so that poor Colby won't make it to land. I couldn't have him spoiling my revenge. I know that there is a difference between a turtle dove and a turtle, but I had to improvise here and there to make all of this work.

SARAH: You're the killer!

ELLA: Pieced that together, did you?

(She pulls an oddly shaped knife out of the Christmas tree.)

Like this. I had this made special. It's a knife with a partridge for a handle. And see those little pear ornaments? I put those there myself. I put up all of these decorations.

SARAH: How?

ELLA: I paddleboarded out to the island on a nice day. Everything is so secluded here, it was easy.

SARAH: But why? Why would you kill your best friends? Why would you do this to us?

ELLA: *(She is crazy:)* Why? That's a good question, Sarah, and since it's only you and me here, I guess I can answer that for you. We have plenty of time, you know. Have a seat, would you?

SARAH: Why?

ELLA: Because if you don't, I'll just stab you now and get it over with.

(Sarah sits.)

Good girl. You remember how much I was against stealing the money for the shelter?

SARAH: I do. We both were.

ELLA: And I wanted to tell the principal, but you talked me out of it.

SARAH: I shouldn't have done that.

ELLA: You're darn right you shouldn't have!

SARAH: *(Starting to panic:)* I'm sorry.

ELLA: It's too late for that now! What you didn't know…what no one knew was that I had been hired on by the Parker Center two weeks before the money went missing. I was set to start January 3rd.

SARAH: I had no idea.

ELLA: It was my dream job! But when the money disappeared, my job offer was revoked. Apparently, a good portion of my salary was to come from the very money my friends stole.

SARAH: That sucks.

ELLA: Tell me about it.

SARAH: But all of this…

ELLA: Yes?

SARAH: It seems a bit much…

ELLA: DOES IT?! Does it seem a bit much to you, Sarah?!

SARAH: You killed 10 people.

ELLA: I've been planning this since January. Figuring out how to make each of you pay for stealing Christmas from the needy…for taking away my dream of helping people.

SARAH: You could still help people…

ELLA: I wanted to get paid to do it!

SARAH: Oh. OK…

ELLA: Is that too much to ask for, Sarah? Is that too much?!

SARAH: I guess not…

ELLA: And you guys never even checked on Jacob. I set that one up really cleverly.

SARAH: OK…

ELLA: Don't you want to know how I made it fit into the song?

SARAH: Not really.

ELLA: FINE! I'll stab you now then!

SARAH: I changed my mind. How did you fit it in?

ELLA: I stole four cell phones.

SARAH: Right. I knew that.

ELLA: Last week I sent you all a text that had a picture of a penguin holding a telephone, remember?

SARAH: Yeah, I remember.

ELLA: So, I put that pic as the background on their phones and left them on Jacob's body after I beat him to death with a two-by-four.

SARAH: You beat him to death with a two-by-four?

ELLA: You're focusing on the wrong part of the story. I left four CALLING BIRDS on his body.

(She starts to laugh maniacally.)

Although, I had to draw a bird on Malik's phone because it was dead.

SARAH: But why?

ELLA: Because his phone was dead, Sarah!

SARAH: I mean, why kill us? How are you going to get away with it?

ELLA: Well, after I finish you off with my partridge in a pear tree, I plan to retrieve the paddleboard I left at the neighbor's house and paddle out of here.

SARAH: But they'll catch you.

ELLA: They'll think I'm dead just like you are, and by the time they figure it out, I will have crossed the border and be on my way to Guatemala.

SARAH: Guatemala?

ELLA: I have a friend there who owns a butcher shop.

SARAH: Do you even speak Spanish?

ELLA: I'll learn! But enough wasting time. Time for me to finish my song!

(She menacingly crosses to Sarah.)

THREE FRENCH HENS, TWO TURTLE DOVES...

(At this, Colby appears with Nick's baton in hand and strikes Ella hard at the base of her head.)

COLBY: And a partridge in a pear tree!

(Lights fade and come up, and Colby is now addressing a police officer who is interrogating him. He gives this speech toward the audience.)

No, I promise, officer. I totally said that when I hit her in the head. I know, I was impressed with myself, too. I had no idea that hitting her that hard would put her in a coma, though. I'm sure when she wakes up, you will be able to get all of this out of her yourself, right? So, basically, I got about thirty minutes into the water and knew I couldn't make it, so I turned around. The raft was starting to sink. I barely made it back in time to hear the end of Ella's speech. I had the baton on me, and, well, I did what I did. Sarah backed me up on all of this, right?

(Gets a reply.)

OK, good. It was pretty horrible.

(Listens.)

Look, it wasn't my idea to move the bodies around! Weren't you listening? Yeah, looking back, I guess I could have stopped them, but I was kinda trying to not get killed, ya know? I do have a question, though, that's been bugging me. I'm hoping you can answer it, what with being a police officer and all.

(He gets consent.)

OK. So, when people die, what percentage of them...ya know... poop themselves?

(Blackout. End of play.)

The Author Speaks

What inspired you to write this play?

Originally it was going to be a Christmas play for my honors class at Laney High School, but when I started writing it, the show turned into a play that has a Christmas theme but actually takes place later in the year. As with most of my shows, I write for the kids I teach, and I immediately produce the shows with that class.

Was the structure or some other element of the play influenced by any other work?

The show is influenced by my love of Agatha Christie's *Ten Little Indians*, which I performed with Laney High School back in the 1990s. I took that show and mashed it up with the lyrics of "The Twelve Days of Christmas" and came up with the idea of killing the students off that way.

Have you dealt with the same theme(s) in other works that you have written?

This is my first murder mystery, but I do write a lot of comedies, and many of them are as irreverent as this one. I happened to get lucky and have twelve students in my honors class the semester I wrote this, or I would have had to change the theme entirely.

What writers have had the most profound effect on your style?

I have been directing shows for years and have always enjoyed Don Zolidis, Jason Pizzarello, Ian McWethy, Peter Bloedel and many others. Don Zolidis was particularly helpful when I decided to get my own work published, and I appreciate the time he took to answer my questions when I was literally clueless.

What were the biggest challenges involved in the writing of this play? For example, was there a particular moment that was difficult to write, and if so, why?
Coming up with how to incorporate deaths to the lyrics of the song! Holy cow, that took some time, and I had to cheat once or twice. (Nine ladies dancing in particular.) Coming up with a few of the deaths was easy, but the more I wrote, the trickier it got. Also, finding motivation to keep splitting up the group and isolating victims was tough, and eventually I had to give up a bit of realism in doing so.

What is your playwriting "origin story"?
I got tired of trying to find shows to fit the kids I teach! It honestly became easier to write a show that fit the 13 girls and 3 guys I had in a class than to find a show that has that many roles in that gender order and with each role having enough lines and action to allow a student to grow as a performer. It took me less than two years of teaching to get tired of the search and start doing it myself.

How did you research the subject? Are any characters modeled after real life or historical figures?
This show was written for the twelve kids I taught the semester we performed it. I wrote in their voices (but exaggerated) and did my best to stay true to the dynamic that class had. I will note that these kids are all wonderful people and would never steal money from a homeless shelter! Also, Ella, the murderer, is a particularly sweet person, so making her the killer was a lot of fun.

What is your writing process?
I would love to be the type of person who can write a little every day, but I can't. I write when the spirit moves and then go through droughts of nothing at all. I wrote this show, like I do most of my shows, from start to finish in a couple of days. My kids help me by reading it as I write and help me edit out the

countless typos. Sometimes I can write three shows in a month, and sometimes I can't write a thing for months on end. I guess I'm weird.

Shakespeare gave advice to the players in Hamlet; if you could give advice to your cast, what would it be?
Enjoy yourselves onstage. Let go of reality and enjoy the irreverence for death and the fact that these kids seem to shrug off their friends dying brutally. But take it seriously! The more serious you are in the moment, the funnier it will be to the audience!

How was the first production different from the vision that you created in your mind?
I had a feeling it was going to be a lot of fun, but it was even better than I hoped. The audience really loved the comical brutality of the show. Of course, I had great performers that added so much to this piece, and that helped a ton. They gave me ideas in direction that made their way into the final script.

When you're not writing, what might we find you doing?
I play a lot of video games, and I have a garage full of 1980s and 90s arcade cabinets that I have repaired over time. I run a martial arts school and enjoy that, but my favorite gig is being a dad. Getting into mischief and going on adventures with my son Rhett is the best.

What was your favorite death in this show?
My answer would be when they found the note on Jackson's back for nine ladies dancing. I had racked my brain trying to figure out a way to make that one work in the script and came up with nothing. With that in mind, I came up with the idea that the killer would have had the same problem!

About the Author

Brent Holland teaches theatre at Laney High School (his alma mater) in Wilmington, North Carolina. He started writing for his "drama kids," but now his plays have been performed all over the U.S. and internationally. Having also taught Physical Education, he is a high-ranking black belt in Isshin-Ryu Karate, having trained since childhood and owning his own dojo since 2001. When not at Laney or the dojo, Brent enjoys spending time with his family, working on old arcade machines and surfing.

About YouthPLAYS

YouthPLAYS (www.youthplays.com) is a publisher of award-winning professional dramatists and talented new discoveries, each with an original theatrical voice, and all dedicated to expanding the vocabulary of theatre for young actors and audiences. On our website, you'll find one-act and full-length plays and musicals for teen and pre-teen (and even college) actors, as well as duets and monologues for competition. Many of our authors' works have been widely produced at high schools and middle schools, youth theatres and other TYA companies, both amateur and professional, as well as at elementary schools, camps, churches and other institutions serving young audiences and/or actors worldwide. Most are intended for performance by young people, while some are intended for adult actors performing for young audiences.

YouthPLAYS was co-founded by professional playwrights Jonathan Dorf and Ed Shockley. It began merely as an additional outlet to market their own works, which included a substantial body of award-winning published and unpublished plays and musicals. Those interested in their published plays were directed to the respective publishers' websites, and unpublished plays were made available in electronic form. But when they saw the desperate need for material for young actors and audiences—coupled with their experience that numerous quality plays for young people weren't finding a home—they made the decision to represent the work of other playwrights as well. Dozens and dozens of authors are now members of the YouthPLAYS family, with scripts available both electronically and in traditional acting editions. We continue to grow as we look for exciting and challenging plays and musicals for young actors and audiences.

About ProduceaPlay.com

Let's put up a play! Great idea! But producing a play takes time, energy and knowledge. While finding the necessary time and energy is up to you, ProduceaPlay.com is a website designed to assist you with that third element: knowledge.

Created by YouthPLAYS' co-founders, Jonathan Dorf and Ed Shockley, ProduceaPlay.com serves as a resource for producers at all levels as it addresses the many facets of production. As Dorf and Shockley speak from their years of experience (as playwrights, producers, directors and more), they are joined by a group of award-winning theatre professionals and experienced teachers from the world of academic theatre, all making their expertise available for free in the hope of helping this and future generations of producers, whether it's at the school or university level, or in community or professional theatres.

The site is organized into a series of major topics, each of which has its own page that delves into the subject in detail, offering suggestions and links for further information. For example, Publicity covers everything from Publicizing Auditions to How to Use Social Media to Posters to whether it's worth hiring a publicist. Casting details Where to Find the Actors, How to Evaluate a Resume, Callbacks and even Dealing with Problem Actors. You'll find guidance on your Production Timeline, The Theater Space, Picking a Play, Budget, Contracts, Rehearsing the Play, The Program, House Management, Backstage, and many other important subjects.

The site is constantly under construction, so visit often for the latest insights on play producing, and let it help make your play production dreams a reality.

More from YouthPLAYS

The Best Drama Club Fundraiser of All Time, Minus That Part Where We Accidentally Summoned a Demon by Brent Holland
Comedy. 35-40 minutes. 7 females, 3 males, 1+ any (11 performers, plus unlimited optional extras).

When the drama club's annual haunted house fundraiser tanks, it appears all is lost. Or it would be if the stage manager hadn't discovered an ancient copy of the *Necronomicon* and, with an assist from his best friend, accidentally summoned a demon. With a little "help," the haunted house becomes the success of a lifetime, but there's one big problem: the department is now stuck with a demon...a demon that has no intention of leaving!

A (Very Zombie) Christmas Carol by Steph DeFerie
Horror Comedy. 25-30 minutes. 2 females, 4 males, 2-6+ any gender (8-12+ performers possible).

In this twisted take on the well-loved Christmas tale, Scrooge not only has to contend with ghosts trying to save his soul but also zombies trying to eat his brains. Thank goodness Bob Cratchit and his family are armed to the teeth and ready to mow down the undead. Christmas is indeed shaping up to be the most wonderful—and bloodiest—time of the year.

An Avalanche of Murder by Matt Buchanan
Comic Mystery. 75-85 minutes. 8-12 females, 4-7 males (13-16 performers possible).

In this affectionate spoof of old-fashioned murder mysteries, the Hopkins family is trapped in a house by a freak avalanche, and they're dropping like flies. It's up to young Mary and Anthony to figure out who's killing them off one by one—and bragging about it on a dead phone—before there's nobody left.

Alice's Christmas in Wonderland by Tommy Jamerson
Comedy. 55-60 minutes. 3 females, 3 males, 15+ any gender (21-30+ performers possible).

When Alice doesn't receive the doll she desperately wants for Christmas, she wishes herself to the one place she believes will be filled with holiday cheer: Wonderland...only to discover her favorite holiday has been banned by the Queen of Hearts. It's up to Alice to save the day once more and teach her fantastical companions a thing or two about the joy of giving to others—but she'll first have to grow up a little along the way.

Best Foot Forward by Lojo Simon & Brandon Scott Grayson
Musical. 45-55 minutes. 2-8 gender-flexible performers.

Eleven-year-old Colorado farmkid Sawyer McNally dreams of showing off their tap-dancing skills in Denver's Dance Starz regionals—but "Lil G" González wows the judges with their hip-hop routine and wins the coveted first-place crown, devastating Sawyer. Will these rivals let their differences divide them? Or maybe they'll discover they have more in common than they expected in this bilingual musical that weaves together styles of music, dance and culture, encouraging friendship across boundaries of geography, language and experience.

Youth on the Outs(ide) by Laura King
Performable Collection. 60-70 minutes. 3-13 females, 1-9 males (4-16 performers possible).

As they navigate high school life in boatyards, graveyards and elsewhere in the great (or not so great) outdoors, the teens in these six short plays find themselves exploring unfamiliar territory—all the while learning that sometimes it's okay to wander off the beaten path to discover where you need to go.

Made in the USA
Columbia, SC
12 October 2024